SABRINA

The Girl With A Hole In Her Heart

Written By Wendy Lewis & Illustrated By Diane Lucas

Tel Aviv, Israel

Zanzibar

Based On A True Story Of Hope And Big Hearts

Two Dolphins Publishing Group

For Steven and Daniel
Who make my heart whole in so many ways

PRONUNCIATION GUIDE AND VOCABULARY

Amharic	(Am-HER-ik)	Semitic language that is the official language of Ethiopia
Catheter	(KATH-i-ter)	A long, thin, flexible, hollow tube that can be inserted into the heart
Duma	(DO-ma)	Swahili word for "cheetah"
Hevi	(HE-ve)	Iraqi girl's name that means "hope"
Jambo	(JOM-bo)	"Hello" in Swahili
Israel	(IZ-ree-uhl)	100th smallest country, leader in medical and technology advances
Kibbutz	(Ki-BOOTS)	A farm or community in Israel where people live and work together
Lev	(Lev)	"Heart" in Hebrew
Mkubwa	(m-CUBE-wa)	An "important or great person" in Swahili
Mnazi Mmoja	(m-NA-zee MO-ja)	"One Coconut" in Swahili, the name of a hospital
Red Colobus	(KOL-uh-buhs)	Endangered species of African monkeys with silky reddish-brown fur
Shalom	(SHAH-lohm)	Hebrew word that means "hello," "goodbye," and "peace"
Sivan	(SI-von)	A girl's name in Hebrew; also the third month of the Jewish calendar
Zanzibar	(ZAN-zi-bar)	A collection of islands (archipelago) in the Indian Ocean, off the East African Coast

Photo credits: P. 12, Echocardiogram with ASD, ColorFlow Doppler-Knol, Dr. Thomas Bashore, Atrial Septal Defect [Internet]. Version 14. Knol. 2008 Jul 22. http://knol.google.com/k/thomas-bashore/atrial-septal-defect/m8O9GE8W/t187fQ. P. 20, Esty Lomas, M.A. Movement Therapist, SACH. P. 31, Diagram of Heart with ASD, © 2011 W.L. Gore & Associates.

Library Control Card No. 2011927761
ISBN: 978-0-615-47819-7

Summary: Sabrina, a 10-year-old girl from a village in Zanzibar travels to another country for a life-saving heart surgery. Based on the work of Save A Child's Heart. 1. Multicultural-Juvenile Literature 2. Human Anatomy- Heart and Heart Defects –Juvenile Literature 3. Humanitarianism-International Cooperation to save children's lives-Juvenile Literature 4. Israel-Juvenile Literature 5. Zanzibar- Africa- Juvenile Literature 1. Lewis, Wendy 2. Lucas, Diane, ill. II. Title.

*Special thanks to Professor James Houser at Baylor University;
to Dr. Daniel S. Levi, Pediatric Cardiologist, Mattel Children's Hospital at UCLA;
and to Suzi, Dennis, Teri, Marcia, Nancy, Lenora, and Kamryn.*

Dear Readers:

How would you feel if you couldn't run or jump or play because you had a heart defect? What if your family didn't have enough money to pay for your much-needed surgery and your country didn't have doctors who could help? Now imagine a humanitarian organization of medical volunteers who travel to countries all over the world to screen children, repair their hearts, and train other doctors for free. The name of this remarkable organization is Save a Child's Heart (SACH).

The story of Sabrina, a fictional character, represents the experience of over 2,600 children from more than forty-three developing countries to date who have been healed by Save a Child's Heart.

In writing this story, I learned the true meaning of humanitarianism from Simon Fisher, the Executive Director of SACH, whom I first spoke to at four a.m. (his time!) while he was at Ben Gurion Airport picking up two surgeons from Vietnam and China; from Sheila, who graciously shared stories of her medical missions to Zanzibar; from Laura, the SACH housemother; from Esty, the Dance and Movement Therapist; and from the stories of the children themselves.

Please enjoy this story of hope and big hearts!

Wendy Lewis

"Wake up, Sabrina. The radio call has gone out.

The foreign doctors are here!"

I know I should get up. This is important news.

But instead of listening to mother, I pull the covers tightly over my head.

I wait patiently for the roosters' crow and the monkeys' chatter.

They are silent so I fall back asleep.

In my dreams, I am running on sandy, coconut tree beaches.

I smell the cinnamon, nutmeg, vanilla, and cloves—the scents of our African Spice Islands, and I feel calm again.

In my dreams, I am *duma*, the cheetah, who outruns any boy on the soccer field until I wake up and remember the day when my chest felt heavy.

After three or four steps, I had to squat down low to catch my breath.

I tried to take one more step, and I . . .

C O L L A P S E D.

Mother rushed me to Mnazi Mmoja hospital to see the local doctor from our village, Dr. Kissanga.

"Nadhifa, something is wrong with Sabrina's heart and maybe her lungs. I don't have the training to properly diagnose her, but I read in the European newspapers about other doctors who might be able to help. They travel to developing countries around the world. They volunteer their time and their surgeries are free. I will invite them to Zanzibar right away."

Now, two weeks later, the Save a Child's Heart doctors (SACH) from Israel have arrived.

At the hospital courtyard more and more families join us as we line up. By daybreak it seems as if the whole island is here.

After waiting six hours, I am exhausted, but I finally hear my name.

"*Jambo*, Sabrina. I am Dr. Lev, and I will be doing an evaluation of your heart."

WELCOME SAVE A CHILD'S HEART DOCTORS

Soon, nurses are swabbing cold gel on my chest and attaching sensors that look like small circles with wires to a 3-D echo machine. Dr. Lev waves a special wand over my chest that sends sound waves to his laptop computer to create an image of my heart. Pointing to a spot on the black and white image, he shows my mother where I have a large hole between the right and left chambers of my heart.

"Because of that hole, Sabrina is not getting enough oxygen to her lungs and the rest of her body, and that is why she is so weak. She should have had surgery when she was six months old, but I think I can repair the hole," says Dr. Lev.

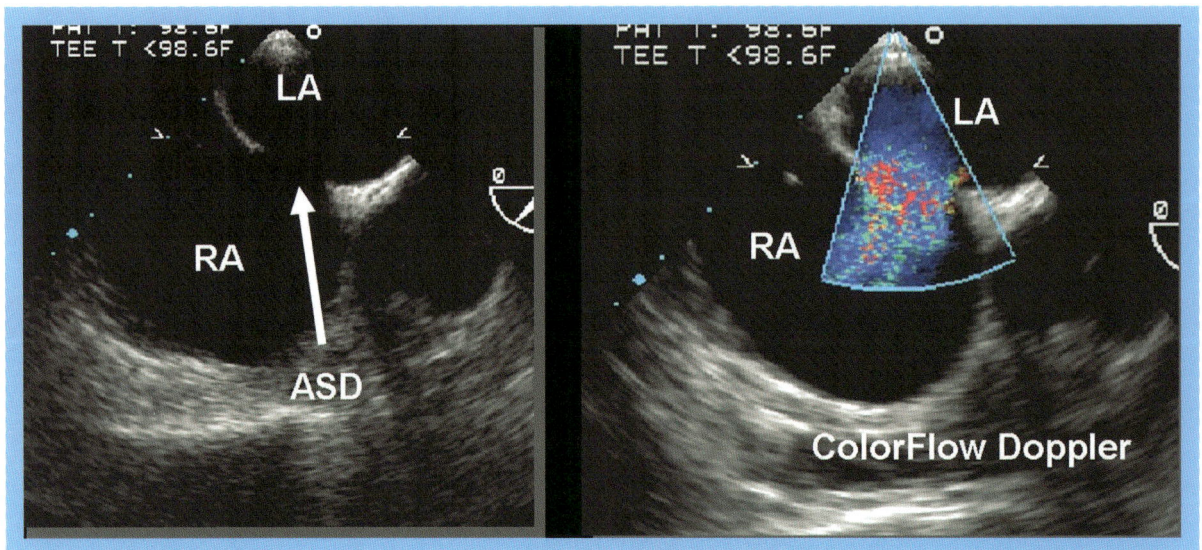

The first image is a real Echocardiogram showing a hole in the heart or ASD (Atrial Septal Defect). The second image, the Colorflow Doppler, helps the doctor to see how blood is flowing through the hole.

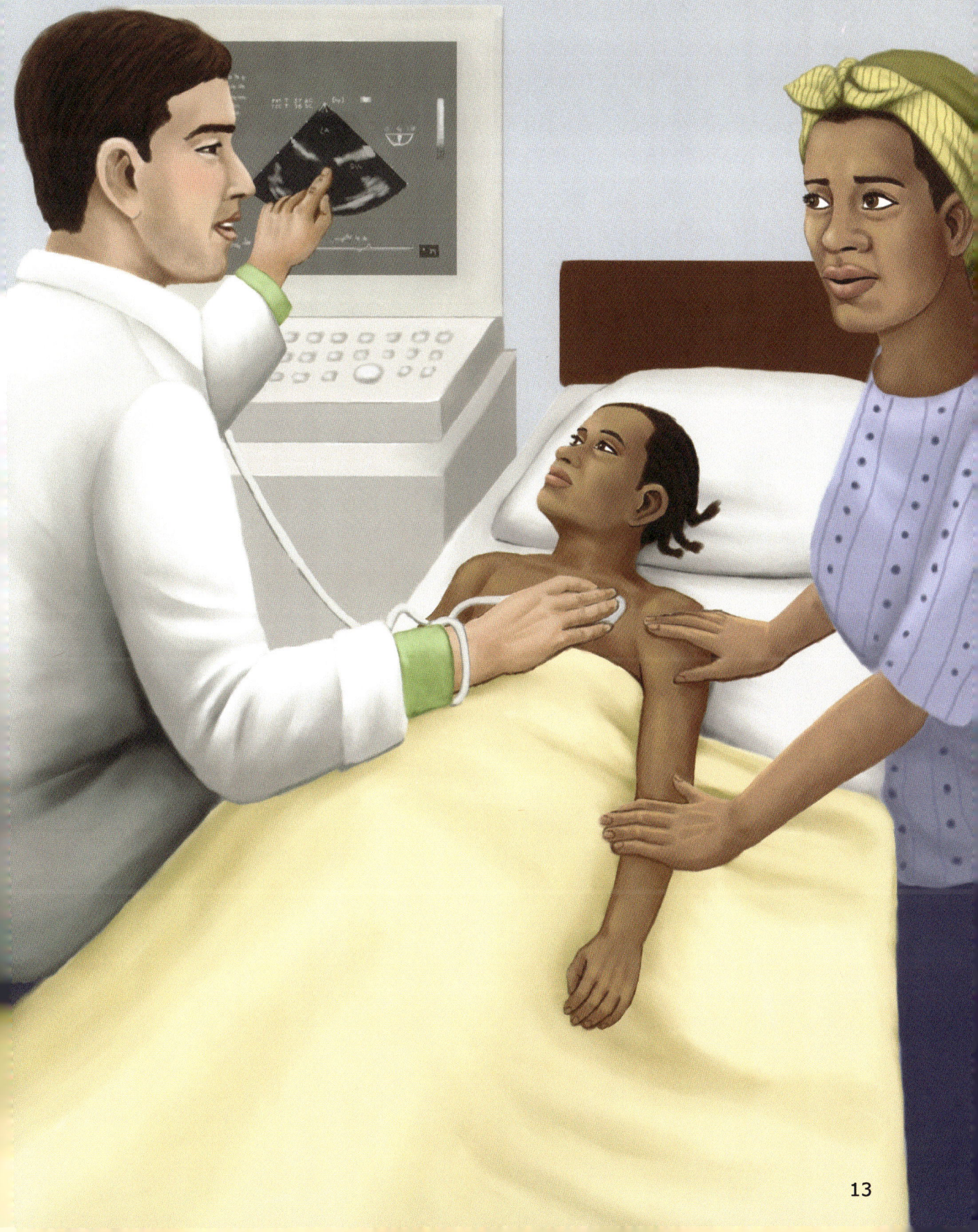

That night, I toss and turn in my sleep. These doctors are not from Africa, and to receive their surgery I will have to leave my village and fly alone on a big bird to a faraway place.

I hear the voices of my mother and big brother.

"But, mother, how can you let Sabrina go?"

"These doctors have a very high success rate, Mkubwa. If your sister doesn't have the surgery, she may not celebrate her next birthday. What choice do we have?"

And now, the thought of *not* going scares me even more.

Ten days later, mother drives me to the airport and gives me a photo with a good luck present wrapped in a big silver box.

Mother whispers, "Be brave, my daughter. These doctors will take better care of you than I."

I choke back the tears and look away. Sivan, an Israeli girl, carries my suitcase and gently takes my hand. On the plane, she wraps an extra blanket and her arms around me, until I fall asleep.

The next morning we arrive at Ben Gurion Airport in a place called Tel Aviv, Israel. At the airport, doctors check us to make sure we are still fine. One boy is taken directly to a hospital while the rest of us board a bus to the Save a Child's Heart house, where I meet children from all over the world.

We put our bags down, eat, rest, and are given new clothes. Some of the children really need them.

Slava, who comes all the way from Russia, carries a plastic bag with only one shirt, while two boys from Ethiopia wear clothes that are full of holes.

How strange, I think. Even though I live in a thatch and mud hut, at least I have enough to eat, and my clothes are always colorful and neat.

"Say hello to Hevi, your roommate. She is from northern Iraq," says Sivan.

I smile at Hevi but she just stares at the walls. All of a sudden, I hear a giant sob, and Hevi is clutching the photo on my nightstand of my brother and me. I want my photo back, but before I can grab it Hevi goes to her drawer. She pulls out a photo of her own.

I count three sisters and two brothers.

And finally one big smile on Hevi's face.

Then Hevi takes me by the hand. She leads me to the window and points to a beautiful desert park below. From our room, I can see children swinging happily on swing sets and sliding down a yellow slide. They remind me of the monkeys at home, the red colobus who are very social and love to play.

I wonder, will that ever be me?

The week before our surgeries, Sivan takes us to the hospital for our tests. I don't like needles, so I look at the pretty coral fish tanks and try to be brave for Hevi's sake.

Later, we visit Leah, the therapist, who helps us understand our upcoming surgeries and express ourselves using communication boards.

homesick

SWAHILI: HAMU YA KWENDA NYUMBANI

ARABIC: بدي أزوح على البيت
BEDI AROH ALA BAIT

AMAHARIC: ﻒﭼﻚﺌﺙﺂﻚ
(Nafi Kaalo)

ﺗﻤﻮﻥ ﺑﺮﻡ ﺑﯚ ﻣﺎﻟﺎﻭﺭ:
AMAWIA BROM BO MAALAWA

These are real communication boards used by SACH therapists.

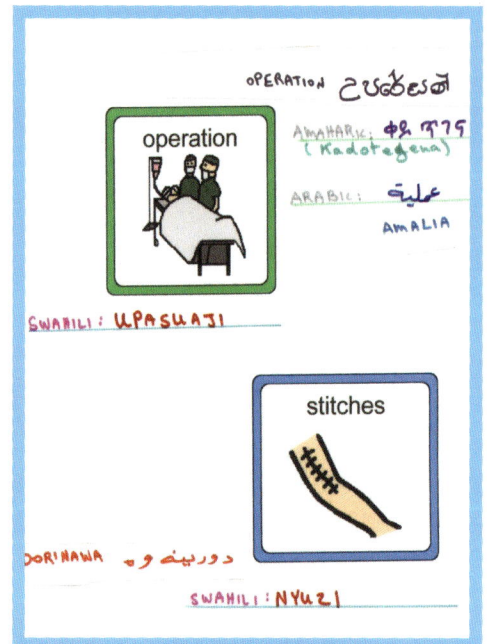

OPERATION ఎ౭ధ్డెండొడి

operation

AMAHARIC: ᎦᏛᎿᎿᎿᎿᎿ
(Kadotegena)

ARABIC: عمليه
AMALIA

SWAHILI: UPASUAJI

stitches

DORINAWA دوربينه و

SWAHILI: NYUZI

We also enjoy fun activities, too.

Volunteers from America teach us about photography and give me my first camera. Students from Canada dress up as clowns while two Israeli teenagers bring toys and teach me how to type on a computer.

The day of my surgery Dr. Lev stops by our room.

"Sabrina, your tests are very good. Any questions before we begin?"

I say nothing, but Dr. Lev is like my brother Mkubwa and can sense my mood.

"Come on, Sabrina." Dr. Lev smiles and looks kindly into my eyes. "All of the children have lots of questions before their surgery."

"What happened to the boy? The one who went to the hospital at the airport?" I finally ask.

"He is doing fine. He already had his surgery, and will be back at the SACH house in one week," answers Dr. Lev.

I feel happy and relieved to hear that, but there is still something else that terrifies me. I bite my tongue once before I speak.

"Dr. Lev, one of the boys says during the surgery you will stop my heart so you can close the hole. And while you are operating, a machine will pump my blood?"

That's true," says Dr. Lev. He takes out a piece of paper and draws a picture of a heart lung machine, an equal sign, and a heart.

"But what if the electricity goes out like in Zanzibar? What will happen to me?"

"No worries, Sabrina. We have a back-up generator that can make electricity for the entire hospital so the heart-lung machine will always work."

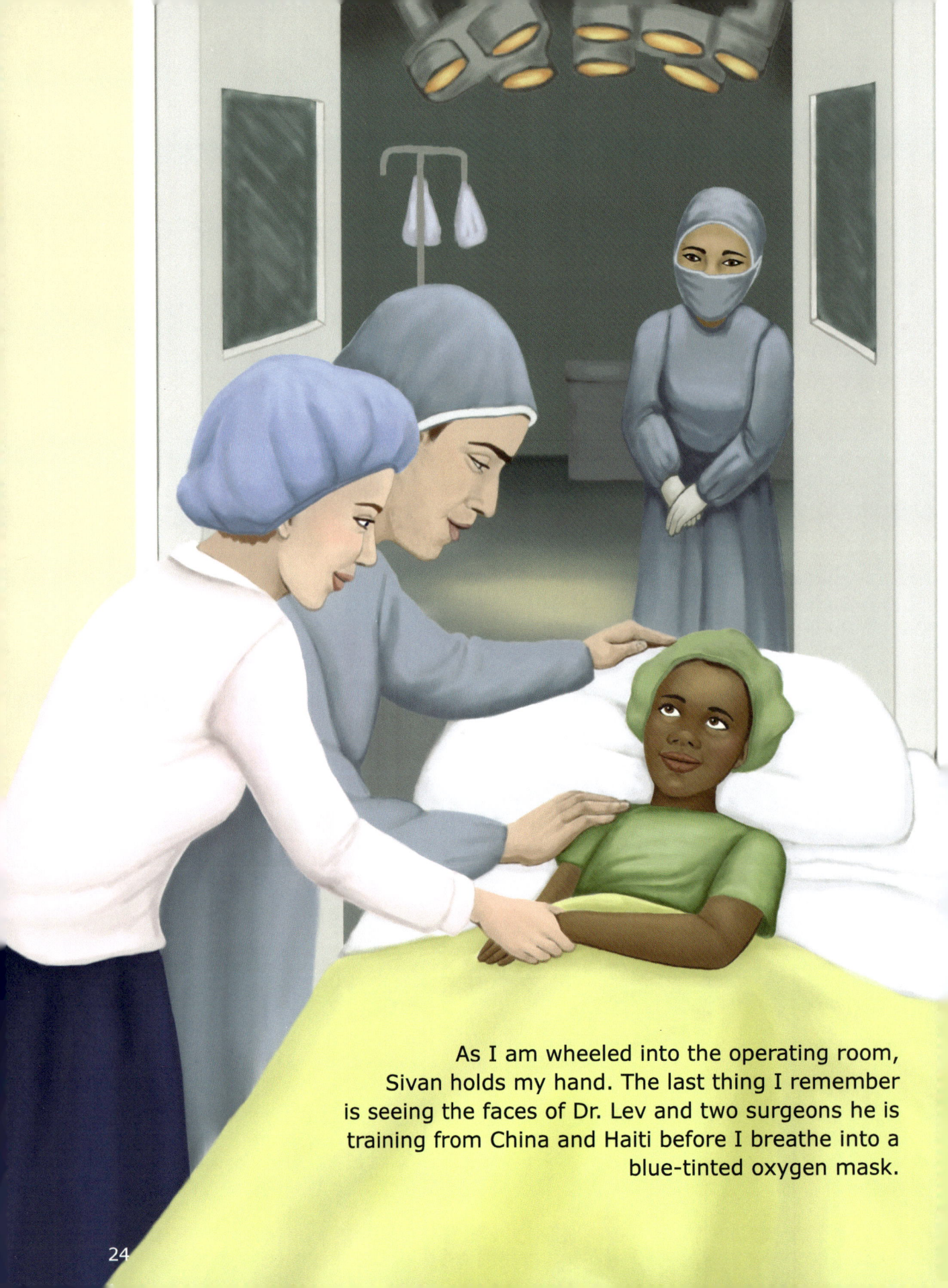

As I am wheeled into the operating room, Sivan holds my hand. The last thing I remember is seeing the faces of Dr. Lev and two surgeons he is training from China and Haiti before I breathe into a blue-tinted oxygen mask.

When I awake, I look like a fighter pilot—still wearing an oxygen mask that is connected to miles of tubes, sensors, and tape.

Soon, Dr. Lev comes by to check my heart.

"Sabrina, your surgery was a success. We repaired the hole, and you now have a healthy heart!"

Then Dr. Lev hands me his cell phone. It is my mother! She says that she loves me, and for the first time, I start to cry.

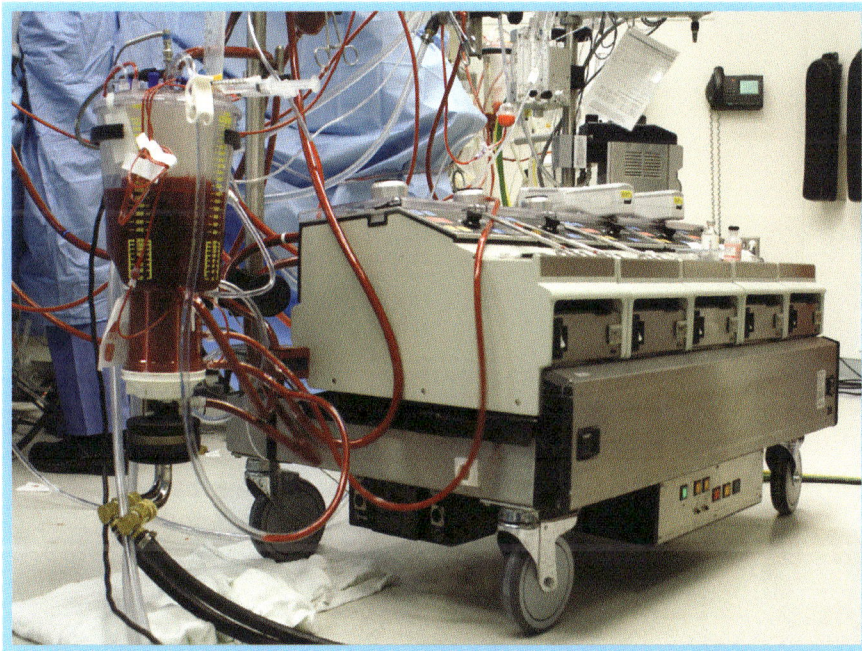

*During surgery, the **Heart-Lung machine** takes over the function of the heart and lungs. The machine takes oxygen poor blood from the heart, adds oxygen, and then pumps oxygen-rich blood to the body.*

Five weeks after my surgery, I finally heal and am strong enough to leave the SACH house and fly back home. But five of the other Zanzibari children are still recovering, so I have to wait.

The next weeks fly by very fast. Hevi and I get up every morning, and after breakfast we race to the park. We kick the soccer ball, the gift from my mother, with new friends from many parts of the world. Even though some of us speak Swahili while others speak Amharic, English, Russian, Arabic, Spanish, or Chinese, we all play together very well.

Two days before my flight back home, Sivan stops by my room.

"Sabrina, would you like to see some of my country? Dr. Lev said you are making a remarkable recovery and you could spend the day with me."

I am so excited that I jump up and down. Then I sit and think. Is this healthy girl really me?

The next morning Sivan drives me to the lowest point on earth, the Dead Sea.

I dip my feet into the sea where Cleopatra used to bathe and take pictures of Sivan floating in very salty water where she can't sink.

Next we go for a camel ride, and Sivan yells, "Watch out for camel spit!"

We have a late lunch at Sivan's kibbutz where I milk a cow and pick a watermelon for dessert.

When we return to the Save a Child's Heart home, I can't believe what I see. The desert park is lit up, and waiting is a world village of people who care deeply about me.

"*Shalom*, Sabrina," yell the other children, nurses, volunteers, Dr. Lev, and other doctors who are already sitting at long tables with vegetables, fruits, and platters of food.

I shout back, "*Shalom*" to say hello, goodbye, and peace.

Dr. Lev gives me a beautiful heart necklace and then I sit with my new friends. As I look around the table, I think, *To save a child is to save a world.*

When I emerge from the plane, my mother is in tears as she sees me walking down the ramp and carrying my own suitcase for the very first time.

Thanks to the doctors in my second home,
Each day I get stronger, and once again,
I am *duma.*

I run like the cheetah.

Jambo and *Shalom*.

Sabrina

MORE ABOUT THE CHILDREN AND SAVE A CHILD'S HEART

True or False Quiz
(Just For Fun! You Won't Be Graded!)

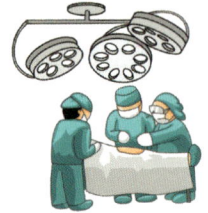

♥ **THE ONLY CHILDREN WHO RECEIVE OPERATIONS COME FROM AFRICA.**

This is false! To date, 2,600 children of all faiths from forty-three developing countries have come to Israel for life-saving heart surgeries. Recently, children from El Salvador, Haiti, Rwanda, Brazil, Iraq, and the Palestinian Authority have been treated by SACH. Can you name some of the countries where children came from in the story?

♥ **THE CHILDREN ARE HARD TO UNDERSTAND BECAUSE THEY SPEAK SO MANY DIFFERENT LANGUAGES.**

This is false! Most of the children travel with an English-speaking nurse or other caregiver who can translate for them. Israel is a country of many cultures. The staff and volunteers at SACH and Wolfson Medical Center where the surgeries take place speak many different languages.

♥ **WHEN A CHILD HAS A HEART DEFECT, IT IS ALWAYS EASY TO GET HELP.**

This is false! Desperate parents often write to SACH and other pediatric heart organizations for help because their country lacks qualified children's heart surgeons, medical facilities, and equipment. Sometimes SACH is the only organization that responds. A family member or doctor may learn about SACH from a news article, like Dr. Kissanga does in the story. Many organizations including hospitals, the Gift of Life International, and Shevet Achim also refer patients to SACH.

♥ **THE CHILDREN OFTEN HAVE ANXIETIES ABOUT THEIR UPCOMING SURGERIES AND ABOUT BEING AWAY FROM HOME.**

This is true! At SACH psychologists, dance and movement therapists, and art therapists use medical play, communication boards, movement, and creative therapies to help the children adjust to their new environment, understand their upcoming medical procedures, and express their feelings about being away from home. This is very important as the average child's stay in Israel is three months.

♥ **SACH PAYS FOR THE SURGERIES SO THERE IS NO CHARGE TO THE CHILD'S FAMILY.**

This is true! SACH must raise $10,000 for each child from donations and supporters. This money covers the cost of the child's hospital stay, local transportation, room, board, recovery at the SACH Children's Home, and other expenses. To keep costs low, Wolfson Medical Center charges SACH the same lump sum fee for operating room use whether the child is in surgery for two hours, ten hours, or has multiple surgeries. Further, SACH doctors and nurses are volunteers who perform the surgeries free of charge.

♥ **ONE OF SACH'S GOALS IS TO TRAIN DOCTORS IN THE DEVELOPING WORLD.**

This is true! The ultimate goal is to provide training, equipment, and supplies to local pediatric cardiologists so they can set up competent medical centers and take care of children in their countries. The SACH doctors, nurses, and staff embrace the Jewish tradition of humanitarianism known as Tikkun Olam (tee-KOON oh LUHM) and believe it is their duty to help repair the world, one child at a time.

♥ **ISRAEL HAS ALWAYS HAD QUALIFIED PEDIATRIC HEART DOCTORS.**

This is false! According to Simon Fisher, the executive director of SACH, just twenty to thirty years ago, Israel was also a developing country and routinely referred her children with heart problems to the United States, Europe, and Canada for diagnosis and treatment. As the country developed, Israel sent its doctors abroad for training and established cutting-edge medical programs at its universities.

♥ **TO LEARN MORE ABOUT SACH:**

Visit www.saveachildsheart.org or contact their offices in Israel: Tel: (972) 3-558-9656, sach@013.net; in the USA: (301) 618-4588, info@saveachildsheartus.org; or in Canada: Tel: (416) 324-9113, info@sachf.ca. SACH also has offices in Australia, France, Germany, Ghana, Holland, Kenya, Switzerland, the United Kingdom, and Vietnam.

ASD, A Hole in the Heart

A Healthy Heart Pumps 2,000 Gallons of Blood a Day!

To the Body: The heart pumps **oxygen-rich blood** from the lungs to the left atrium, then to the left ventricle, and to the rest of your body via the aorta (a main artery).

Back to the Lungs: After your organs and tissues have used the oxygen in your blood, the **blood flows back to your heart, but it is now oxygen-poor** and **carrying carbon dioxide.** The heart pumps the **oxygen-poor** blood from the right atrium to the right ventricle, through the pulmonary artery to the lungs, where it picks up oxygen (while you exhale carbon dioxide), and **the process starts again.**

Make a fist—your amazing heart is just a little larger and does all that!

Some ASDs close on their own while the child is very young. Other ASDs are closed by surgery or by a catheter (KATH-i-ter) based procedure without surgery.

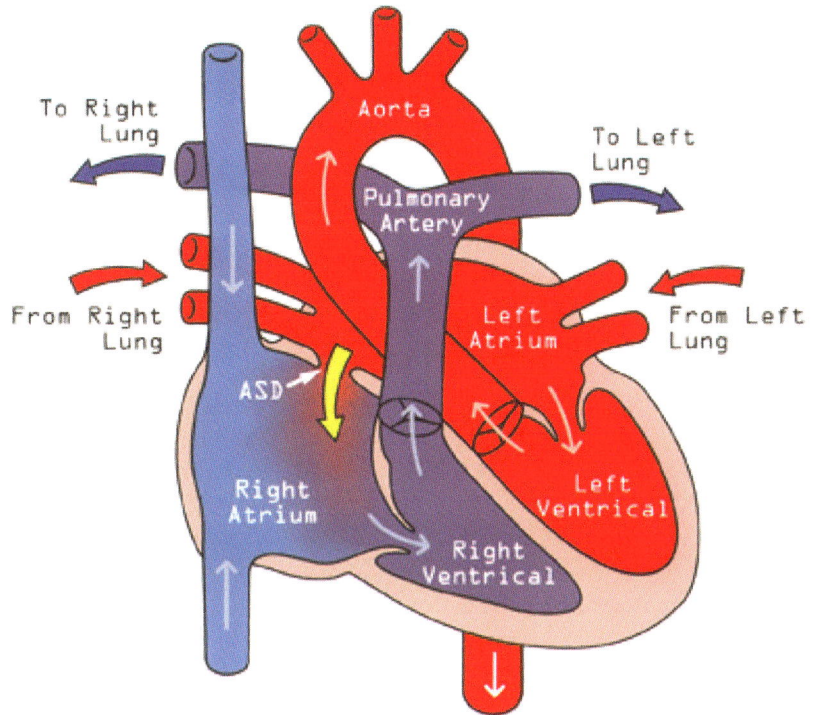

Diagram of Heart with ASD
© 2011 W. L. Gore & Associates, Inc.

ASD (short for Atrial Septal Defect)*

An ASD is a hole or defect in the wall (septum) between the two upper chambers (atria). If a child has this type of hole, what happens to the flow of blood?

Hint: Trace the flow of blood on the diagram. If the hole in the wall is large enough, blood from the left atrium will flow into the right atrium. This creates extra blood flow on the right side of the heart and extra blood flow to the lungs which causes the heart and lungs to work harder. Some children with a hole in the heart may experience no symptoms while other children may easily tire, experience shortness of breath, lung problems, or even congestive heart failure.

*****AY**-tree-uhl **SEP**-tull **DEE**-fect

Lesson Plans Adapted from "The Science Museum of Minnesota/smm.org"

HANDS-ON: MAKE A HEART PUMP

Materials You Will Need:

- Plastic Jar
- Large Balloon
- Bamboo Skewer
- Two Straws that Bend
- Scissor
- Tape
- Container for Water Spills
- Paper Towels for Clean-Up

Procedure: Fill the jar half full of water. Next, cut off the neck of the balloon and save. Stretch the balloon over the top and over the sides of the jar so it forms a seal. With the skewer, poke two small holes into the top, about ¾ inch apart. Insert a straw into each hole. Use the balloon neck to make a valve by taping the neck over the end of one of the straws. Bend down the straw with the valve. Place the jar in the container.

Experiment: Use your fingers to push and release the heart pump several times. What happens to the water? Does it flow through one or both straws? What happens to the flow of water when you remove the balloon flap (the valve) from the pump?

Challenge: What happens during the pumping action of the heart? How do valves affect the flow of blood? Hint: Think of a faucet.

MAKE A STETHOSCOPE

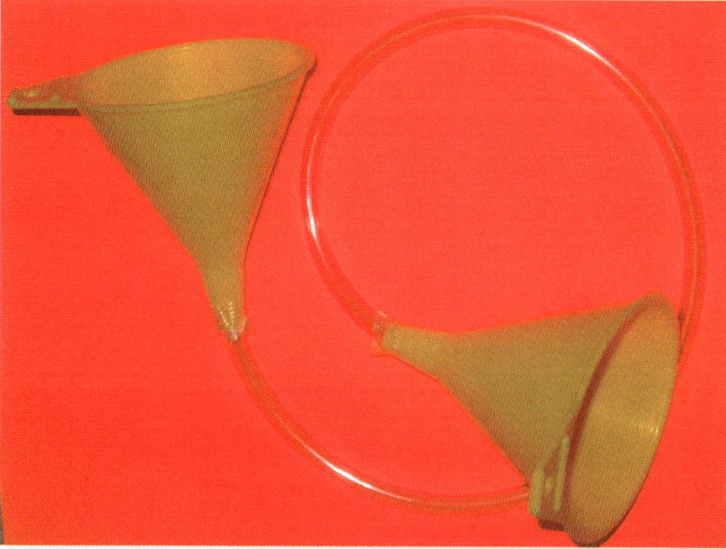

Materials You Will Need:

- Two Funnels
- Two Feet of Plastic Tubing
- Strapping Tape

Procedure: Stick the ends of the tubing ½ inch inside each funnel and tape together on the outside.

Experiment: Hold one of the funnels to your ear and move the other around your chest. Can you hear the "lub dub" sound of your heart? Next, run in place or do jumping jacks for one minute. Use the stethoscope to listen to your heartbeat again. Any change?

Challenge: How does the stethoscope pick up your heartbeat? Hint: Your heartbeat (lub dub lub dub) is the sound (vibrations) of your heart valves closing.

CPSIA information can be obtained
at www.ICGtesting.com
Printed in the USA
262455LV00001B